DIVINE PLACE OF BELONGING

DIVINE PLACE OF BELONGING

DIVINE PLACE OF BELONGING

DANCING ON THE FRINGE OF BELIEVING THERE IS ONE

by
Rev. Clifford J. Viljoen

DIVINE PLACE OF BELONGING

Copyright © 2024 Clifford J. Viljoen

All rights reserved. No part of this publication may be reproduced, distributed. or transmitted in any form or by any means, including photocopying, recording, or other electronic or mechanical methods,
without the prior written permission of the publisher, except in the case of brief quotations embodied in critical reviews and certain other
noncommercial uses permitted by copyright law.

ISBN: 9798869838834 (Paperback)
ISBN: 978-1-7381475-2-6 (eBook)

Scripture quotes taken from the Holy Bible (ESV & MSG Translation)

Front Cover Image by C.J. Viljoen
Book Cover Design by Dania Penney
Printed in the United States of America.
First printing edition 2024.
www.cliffordjviljoen.com

DEDICATION

To my son, Samuel Hezekiah Viljoen,
with great love.

DIVINE PLACE OF BELONGING

Endorsements

"It is a real privilege for me to have been asked to read and endorse Clifford's book. Having known Clifford for around nine years, I can attest to just how much the Lord has done in Cliff's life and in bringing him into a knowledge (lived experience) of the truth of sonship. The first thing that stood out for me as I was reading it, was just how vulnerable and real he has been in describing the journey that he has been on with the Lord. He has not shied away from sharing both the highs and lows of his life but has done it in such a way that gives us a way forward from being orphans and into knowing and experiencing the glorious joy of belonging to, and being with, our heavenly Father. I can wholeheartedly recommend this book as a sound theological and experiential framework for anyone who struggles with knowing their true identity, and for anyone wanting to be reminded of the precious truths of the Gospel."

Murray Hurd

"What a powerful and compelling read. It was a wonderfully storied way of pointing to truth about who God is, and what that means for us. Us being those that are wrestling with belonging, people who have been in the church and are disillusioned towards following God. Rev. Clifford Viljoen writes to shed light on belonging and what that means for the way we live right now."

Brianna Matchett, MC, C.C.C.
Counselling Therapist & Owner
Garden Counselling Services

"It's often difficult to put into words the things the Father has done in one's heart. Yet, at times, a sentence or a picture captures the essence of what you hope will convey what words may not. I believe the words penned on these pages capture the sound and the heart of the Father. A thought that causes your heart to believe that there is a power able to take you beyond your ability to accomplish. This is the sound of the voice of the Father to us all when our hearts may fail us. I encourage you to hoist your sail, just as the writer has done, when you hear the voice of the Father say to you, 'Look my child, here comes the wind.'"

Stephen H. Schroeder
President
Christian Ministers Association of Canada

"To be known, is a deep desire and need of each person. It is a place within each of us that needs to be filled. As you read through these pages, you will quickly become aware of your own position. The questions come up, "Am I known?", "Am I loved?", "Do I belong?" And whether the answer leans toward a yes, then what a beautiful assurance you have. But if the answer leans toward uncertainty, then what a beautiful invitation before you. Clifford so beautifully shares his story as a key to help the reader move from the invitation and into the assurance. A reminder that we need not live in spiritual orphanhood because we have been grafted in."

Angela Viljoen

"Divine Place of Belonging is a call to a place of acceptance: the acceptance of being accepted by the Creator. Honest and raw, Clifford's words remind us of the truth we were all created to live. They are both a reminder and a response to where each of us belong: the heart of the Father who formed us and knit us together. These are words to rest in, to be challenged with, and ultimately to be found in. As you read, don't rush through the words, take your time, and wrestle with them in the depths of you who are."

Alexander Jansen, MC, C.C.C.
Director of Programs & Client Services
Calgary Dream Centre

DIVINE PLACE OF BELONGING

In general, weaving involves using a loom to interlace two sets of threads: the warp which runs longitudinally and the weft that crosses it.

Weft is an Old English word meaning, "that which is woven."

DIVINE PLACE OF BELONGING

Contents

Foreword 15
Introduction: Here Comes the Wind 19

Part I: The Warp

I: Truly Great 25
II: A Room at the Inn 37
III: From the Inside Out 47
IV: Curious Hope 55
V: Well-Informed 63
VI: Wisdom Has Her Reasons 73

Part II: The Weft

VII: Sealing the End of Our Braided Lines 85
VIII: But Would You? 93
IX: Welcome Home 107

DIVINE PLACE OF BELONGING

Foreword

It is a privilege to be given a story that, when reflected upon, fills your heart with delight. We were given such a gift when living in community with Cliff. We had the privilege of sharing a home, many dinners, and Jesus adventures together. The experience inspired us to pursue Jesus, to stand where He stands, and to go where He goes. Together, we found Him standing on the margins, lovingly drawing people to Himself. And in the process of attempting to lift Jesus up, our hearts were changed by Him. We are forever grateful for the story we lived together, and for the many Jesus adventures still to come!

Cliff has a wonderful gift with words and telling stories. We have several Cliff stories that we love to share with friends. What strikes us most about these stories is the way they reflect the heart of a loving Father. A Father so busy loving us, that He has no time to be ashamed of us. Jesus once said, "Those who have been forgiven much, love much." When we think of Cliff, we are reminded of one forgiven much, not because of the many sins that needed forgiving, even though this is true for all of us, but to the degree with which he receives the Fathers love. Cliff has experienced the Father's love and grace at such a high resolution that it pulls one into delight with Jesus. It inspires us to live and serve from delight. Duty can take you some distance, but only delight would have you stand and thrive on the margins.

Cliff is a maker and a thinker. He is outrageously gifted and creative. He is also ruthless in his pursuit of what is true. Because of this, he has a special way of cutting to the heart of an issue with a surgeon's precision. At one stage, Maxie, my wife, and I, lovingly called him our "nonsense" detector. He helped us to not take ourselves too seriously and think deeply about where we find our identity. He helped us remember that people are not projects. He helped us to remember that who we are, and the value we carry, is not limited to the roles we have or the passions we pursue. God deeply invests in shaping us throughout our entire lifetime, reminding us that we are loved children before anything else. This love is not of our own design, but a gift from God.

During our time with Cliff, we also learnt to throw off our culture in pursuit of Jesus. We learnt that many people might really like our Jesus, but that they can't stand us. We will never forget the times when we considered what it meant that our King decided to put on flesh, walk our dusty streets, embrace the leper, sit down with Zacchaeus, and then go on to say, "If you have seen me, you have seen the Father." Together we learnt to look at Jesus, to simply live His life and experience it to be true. To simply point others to Him. He is the only way, and if we have seen Him, we have seen the Father.

We are deeply thankful for the opportunity to contribute to this book. We believe this is an important work, commenting on key issues facing Christian leaders and disciple makers today. If you hope to live a life of delight instead of merely duty, we encourage you to make the most of your spiritual journey by reading and applying the life lessons Cliff shares here.

Marko & Maxie Pretorius

DIVINE PLACE OF BELONGING

Introduction

Here Comes the Wind

As a boy, from time to time, my father would invite me to go sailing with him at the dam. A timber dinghy with two blue sails, a skipper, and I, the crew of one.

There is now a fond persuasion offered to me by literature that speaks of men in their vessels navigating their way by the wind. It captures my attention. It stirs my imagination. That is why when I read what Seneca once wrote, "There is no favorable wind for the sailor who does not know where to go", it took no time at all for imagination to have its way, as I remembered fondly my inexperienced days of crewing for skipper, my father.

Dad was well-versed in reading the wind and knowing where to position himself to use it. So much so, it had earned him the prestigious title of world champion, once upon a time, in both our younger lives. Often in regattas, when the wind would die down, committed skippers would strategically maneuver themselves across the course by jibing, tacking, looking for pockets of wind, faithfully forging forward toward the finish line. Other skippers opted out and headed back to the shoreline.

I'll never forget it. Many had given up in the times of lull. Dad had kept forging forward. Tedious at times, but faithfully, he stayed the course. Then it happened. I could sense something. I was on alert. My attention was drawn. But not by some booming sound or a ringing of an alarm. Rather, it was the tame lapping of the subtle ripples against the dinghy's hull. Then came the cool gentle sensation that embraced my face like that of a loving mother as I looked up to the clouds, swept by the beauty of the blue African sky, unknowing of the impact of this moment and how it would impact my life as an adult man.

My father leaned over and whispered to me, "Look my boy, here comes the wind."

Then, with no permission needed, what delivered the ripples moved swiftly aboard until it had evidently found its way into the sails of our almost stagnant vessel. Seconds later, the sails filled from flapping to full; the dinghy leapt forward, and we were on our way. Dad had faithfully stayed the course, patiently waiting for the wind to return. And when it did, we were right where we needed to be to catch it. We caught the wind, and it carried us home to the finish line.

Many others missed it.

If anything at all, my hope for this simple contribution is that it would serve you in the same way that the wind would serve a sailor that faithfully forges forward toward the finish line. Like a wind that blew in, God sent Ananias to pray for Saul, opening his eyes, filling his sails with the Spirit that would convince him of his sonship and divine place of belonging.

I hope together our eyes open to our true, God-given identities, leading us out from spiritual orphanhood, and into the arms of our loving Father. And from this place, our divine place of belonging, as we endeavor to live out the great call of loving Him, ourselves, and each other, would the same spirit of adoption blow into the sails of our struggling friends a deep sense of sonship.

But primarily, this is for my son, Samuel. This text, as I see it, is something akin to that of the stone monuments that the Israelites erected after crossing through there where they thought they could not. I would like Samuel to know that this union of thought and story is as much his as they are mine.

Dear one, I would like you to know that you have not jeopardized the love that the Father has for you. You are His child, the apple of His eye, and in His heart is your divine place of belonging, where you will find not just any adventure, but your adventure!

May our eyes be opened, and may the wind be found and be favorable as we navigate these challenging times that we are in. As we make our way through the high and the low seas of life, with attention drawn, listening with ears of faith, the ears of our inner heart, let us stay the course, for we shall surely hear,

"Look my child, here comes the wind."

PART I
THE WARP

DIVINE PLACE OF BELONGING

I

Truly Great

Over a fairly long arc of time, a steadily growing list of people have found their names suffixed by the epithet, the great, often because of the manner in which they had led a people, a people they had conquered, or because of some sort of notable contribution to broader society. Scholars have discussed and debated at length the credibility of the title awarded many, but this is not, initially, the focus. For us here on these pages, I offer for your consideration, upon what do we flippantly bestow description such as great? And with that, upon whom do these descriptions belong to then?

Mother Teresa once said, "We cannot all do great things, but we can do small things with great love." These words will land gently on humble hearts, or they may cause a degree of discomfort that, like a fork in the road, force a decision one way or another. While necessary at times, and only for a time, the alternative to deciding to move is to stand still and go nowhere. When moving upon one of the two paths, should we embark with humility, it offers the opportunity to receive from Mother Teresa, and others, such a necessary reminder and encouragement. The other, because there has not yet been an honest account of our own abilities and limitations, we set off in pride, en route to a destination of dislocation from the communities that we move in.

Corrie ten Boom, known for her efforts in helping many Jews escape the Nazi Holocaust during World War II, once said, "If the devil cannot make you bad, he will keep you busy." In the observations that I have made in my life, and in those around me, I find what Corrie says to be strikingly true. However, I offer it differently. If the enemy cannot remove us from the body to which we belong, I suppose the next best thing would be the attempt to dislocate the body part. We need each other. And we need each other to be healthy. What good is the knee when it has been dislocated? You are still part of the body, that is not in question, but a knee that has been dislocated cannot do what it has been made to do in tandem with the rest of the body.

"For just as the body is one and has many members, and all the members of the body, though many, are one body, so it is with Christ. For in one Spirit, we were all baptized into one body—Jews or Greeks, slaves or free—and all were made to drink of one Spirit.

For the body does not consist of one member, but of many. If the foot should say, 'Because I am not a hand, I do not belong to the body,' that would not make it any less a part of the body. And if the ear should say, 'Because I am not an eye, I do not belong to the body,' that would not make it any less a part of the body. If the whole body were an eye, where would be the sense of hearing? If the whole body were an ear, where would be the sense of smell? But as it is, God arranged the members in the body, each one of them, as he chose." (1 Corinthians 12:12-18)

When I think of these two contrasting paths that start at the same place at this proverbial fork in the road, it seems to give bearing to my questioning of what is truly great.

As I hazard to say it differently; because pride tends to pervert our sense of worth, and distorts the way we see the worth of others around us, is it feasible to suggest that an encouragement such as that of Mother Teresa's might well be better, or possibly only, fully understood and received in humility?

You see, in the valiant claims that we make of laying our lives down, pride in all of its deception may not suggest to you to do otherwise. If pride had the ability to twist a noble thought, and it does, let's be clear about that, perhaps it might say lay your life down, but do it for something "great enough." In all of its toxicity, pride might suggest with eloquent deception that your life is worth more than just one other insignificant soul. I've heard it said that in love we are destined for great things, but I fear that "great" may well be misunderstood and think it wise to consider what great is through the lens of humility, because pride will distort what we perceive it to be.

People are searching for greatness. And to reiterate, if our understanding of what great is has been tainted by pride, and with that, if we have mistakenly attached to it our sense of worth, we live trying to prove ourselves, enveloped by insecurity. This has the potential to disable our efforts in loving others well, or at least, blind us to the idea that perhaps the love that has been made known in our own lives has been for the benefit and betterment of another. To the idea that we have been invited into being completely and wholeheartedly there for someone else until they are able to do the same for their neighbor. Are we humble enough to see things not for how great or how small they are, but rather, simply, and in all of its complexity, for who they are!

Why have we allowed the sort of thinking that promotes the idea that we are indeed destined for great things, just as long as they are great enough? I suppose an understandable knee-jerk reaction to that might be, well why not!? Why wouldn't we want to align ourselves with the greatest? That is an appropriate approach to life, and it should be so that we aim for the highest and the best. But what is the highest? What is the best?

What is the greatest? Why is a single life not great enough, important enough, interesting enough? Why would someone else's single life not be worthy of my own being laid down for, unless it comes in multitudes? It is a sobering thought that Jesus had laid His life down for the entire world. But with a refreshed, and more accurate understanding of what great is that comes when we choose not to look through haughty eyes, Jesus astounds us by showing us the kind of humility that the world is begging to see more of.

A single life alone was enough for Him still to do what He did. Yours was and is, utterly enough. I plead with you not to move on too quickly from this old thought that you have surely pondered before. We have heard it from the pulpits. We have heard it in our small groups. We have seen it in our evangelistic endeavors in the pursual of the one lost sheep. It is old, and it is not new. But has it truly taken shape in our lives enough that it would shape the culture around us?

Are you willing to draw from a humble act in history that devastated life as we knew it, ever since it occurred? Would you deeply consider an act in history that has since been lived out by others that have been invited, like you and I have been, to do the same in seeking a renewed understanding of what great truly is?

I remember witnessing a friend come face-to-face with this grapple. It was an incredibly valiant, yet quiet display of honesty and of courage. The fortitude she exhibited when choosing not to glaze over when hearing what she had surely heard so many times before was honorable; that Jesus and the Father would have done for her alone, what They had done for the world that day at Calvary. That was old news for her. Yet that day she chose to consider it anew, or much rather, with a maturity that had been funded by humility that offered a new insight from an event so old.

I had been wondering at that time whether we as a people might have twisted our understanding of what we considered as great and decided to air the question to a group I met with regularly. Unwittingly, this set the table that facilitated a conversation that changed not only my thinking, but also the life of a young boy who was in desperate need.

The friend that I speak of was a highly educated woman. A medical practitioner who dreamed of being on mission with Jesus with her expertise in the dilapidated, war-torn parts of the world. It seemed a great thing to do. She was stirred, but being in her 60s, it scared her, and that had been the reason it seemed too difficult to get out of the boat and onto the water to walk it.

Although the fear had got hold of her, the dream did not diminish. And now, this great dream was in jeopardy. She had been confronted by a still small thought that threatened to devastate this great desire to serve the multitudes. What had been uttered was an invitation to serve "only" one. A young boy in his formative years whose parents felt they could no longer honor the call to be his loving parents while he so desperately needed the love, and at least a parent. That evening in a group setting, this thought was uncomfortably hostile toward what we considered great. Interestingly, the uncomfortable nudge seemed to come with the grace that led our conversation further from one pivotal moment to the next.

There was a tenderness in the room. It was not lost on me, what was at stake. What was the Father doing? To what lengths was the Father willing to go that a child would find his rightful place of belonging? The tension I felt transported me back in time to the first miracle recorded in the Gospel of John. A story told countless times about how the Master spared the newlyweds from the shame and embarrassment that comes as a result of a lack of self-control. They drank freely, without restraint, and the consequence was lack itself. But Jesus produced for this celebration in Cana not what their actions deserved, but over and above what they might have ever asked for. What a stunning display of what Kingdom and grace look like when held up against the rogue ways of the world and the consequences therein.

This ancient story of water being turned into the finest wine was uniquely connected to that which was unfolding in front of me. I felt like I could sense the tension both at the wedding in Cana and in our living room.

Fill the jars with water was Jesus' first request to the servants. So they did. They filled the jars with water. The jar, likened to that of the container of her thoughts, and Jesus' request of "filling it" was an invitation to consider a new thought. So she did. She considered the new and challenging thought. Then, His second request was to draw some water out and take it to the master of the feast. They did. It was water that they drew. Similarly, she drew from the invitation an honest interpretation and shared it with the group for further investigation. Then finally, the concluding request was to deliver the miracle. With these that remain nameless, it is said, simply, that they took it. Now, having delivered what they surely knew was water as they were the faithful servants that filled the jars, I wonder what the anticipation might have felt like as they stood by and witnessed cups of water being raised, lifted to lips, and finally, sampled. It was wine! Imagine the explosive internal exclamations of these servants that delivered the miracle. It is wine! They knew it was water. And now they know it is wine.

When we witness an action that alludes to the label of great, it has caught our attention, and so should beg us the question, who did it? We know that it was Jesus that commanded the miracle, so all credit to Him, but there is something commendable about the unquestionable obedience of the servants who delivered it. In these instances, and there are many, I would feel quite comfortable attaching to these that remain nameless, the epithet that is, the great, because it points us to the One who is truly Great. I would say the same for our friend who filled her jars, drew from them what was asked of her and delivered the miracle of a yes. A yes that gave evidence of the One that is truly Great.

She took the boy in. He found a place of belonging.

It changed this young boy's life. In the Father's eyes, this life was absolutely, and undoubtedly great enough a life for my friend to lay hers down for. And she agreed, because the Father had offered His only Son to death for her, and Jesus willingly agreed to the death and took to the cross for her. But before that decision was made, she traveled through parts of her heart that needed to be looked at. And not just looked at, looked at through humble eyes opened by the blinding light of the crucifixion. On this evening, this strange thought of what is great and the confession of uncertainty around it, pointed us to something truly Great. And it seemed the longer we stared into this blinding light, or pondered it, the more our eyes opened while the rightful things moved into their rightful places, squeezing out any thought that partnered with that of comparison, leaving room for only obedience.

Those ancient words that Jesus later spoke out to the crowds made a way into our living room that evening. We were reminded that the greatest among us did not spend too much time thinking about what is great, He just served. We were reminded that he who exalts himself over another would be humbled. We were reminded that evening that he who bothered not too much about what is great, or what is not, would be found humble. We were also reminded that humility precedes honor.

I said that I had wondered if there might be merit in thinking on what we thought was great. I said that I had recognized that this thought had served as a means to find what is truly Great which suggests that it was a necessary endeavor. But then strangely, I concluded with the peculiar inconsistency that our desire to understand what is great need not be the focus. Instead, would it be voluntary surrender unto the still small thoughts that beckon us to the highest and to the best expression of ourselves amongst others. And to do this with humility as our disposition, knowing that the highest and best expression of self comes by being oriented toward Jesus.

"For this is the will of my Father, that everyone who looks on the Son and believes in him should have eternal life, and I will raise him up on the last day." (John 6:40)

Looking on the Son is being oriented toward Jesus, and putting our belief in Him is being aligned with love. And as I venture to share a curious amalgam of inspired thoughts and story to support this orientation, I must confess that it was not how I had aligned myself for the better part of my life. I have held no issue in believing that Jesus was who He said He was. I, however, had been blind to Him in my own life, and so I struggled to put my belief in Him. For the sake of explanation, one might believe that a surgeon is capable of removing a toxic appendix because that is his qualification and has done it several times before. But it is not until one has put themselves on the operating table and allowed the surgeon to remove the appendix that qualifies their belief in the surgeon. Believing that Jesus is the Son of God differs vastly from that of putting your belief in the Son of God. To add, where you land with this does not remove from Jesus His title, that He is the Son of God. It is the same with us as beloved sons and daughters. Whether you believe that you are a loved son or daughter, or you do not, it does not render the truth of it void. It does, however, dictate to you how you might live your life out.

Gratefully, I have moved from foe to friend of Jesus. And as I walk with Jesus, I am ushered into the heart of the Father. And it is from this place that I offer for your consideration by invitation, would you turn a page and enter into the age-old message of love, sonship, and the prospect of a divine place of belonging.

II

A Room at the Inn

Gazing into the blinding light of the crucifixion was not always a consideration. That is why when I find myself in a moment that reminds me that I have found what it is that I have been looking for all my life, that is belonging, I pause, and I take it in. I remember one evening, my wife and I had ventured out to enjoy a quartet perform "Beethoven's Best Work" in a 110-year-old church. It was sensational. It was not a church event, instead, an event held in a church that no longer operated as one.

Something struck me. It was the colossal, forgotten cross that hung above the musicians. The cross was an icon you would expect to see in a church, and I was compelled to consider it. I was drawn to the cross this evening, but not in the same way as when I had seen this cross being worn by London punks down in Camden Town because it was viewed as edgy, or provocative, to tattoo on your cheekbone, or wear as a pair of earrings. As I sat, exquisitely led by the quartet into a wild and wide range of emotions, pondering this forgotten cross which was something I hadn't fathomed I would come to do so deeply in my life, an extraordinary sense of gratitude gripped me.

Like getting to know a friend, after much time spent together, it is impossible to see just their face when you gaze upon their picture hanging on the living room wall. You see your history with them. In an instant, you remember the moments and the emotions that you experienced with them. The highs. The lows. The victories. The losses. As the years go on in friendship, it seems the picture takes on a weight that once was not there before. That is why, at a glance, a picture can truly be worth a thousand words.

That evening, while it was not the genesis of my relationship with the cross, it was a reflective moment that pointed to it. The cross, now, steadfastly delivers to me a flood of experiences to remember because friendship with the One who hung on it has developed. One such experience I will never forget. I could not carry my weight any longer. It was an onslaught of thought, blatantly aimed at crushing me, until finally I caved and collapsed to my knees. Mercilessly commissioned by the Pacific were the waves that came with a ferocious force. It was as if they beat me into submission as I sank slowly into the black volcanic sands of New Zealand's west coast. An apt representation of what had been unfurling in my head and heart. The palpable soundscape ever adding to the moment. The clouds grew ominously darker, bursting and delivering the last blow like an iron fist, obliterating any last effort to stand. I could not move, and yet, I was powerfully moved by the desperate situation I found myself in.

As I attempted to wrestle myself from the sand, I saw, as in a vision, another man in motion moving with incredible intent. His movements were fluid, and with a dignified elegance about his appearance, he danced around me in the most stunning, radiating white apparel. In grace and perfection of form, he transitioned from a type of pirouette into a glide, instantaneously changing appearance to that of a traditional Zulu warrior. As he pierced the intrusive thoughts in space around me with his spear, and with it emitting a roar so terrifyingly loud, he hushed the raging soundscape that had enveloped me.

"Lift up your spear and javelin against those who pursue me. Let me hear you say, 'I will give you victory!'" (Psalm 35:3)

It gave space for the arrival of a thought unlike all others. It was a thought that rose from deep within. Gently, as it landed on the inner ear of my heart, I heard, "It is finished."

Then, as this mysterious amalgamation of a beautifully curated ballet dance and a scene that seemed to come straight out of an Indlamu Zulu war dance routine unfolded, the ancient echo of the psalmist welled-up; "He shattered the doors of bronze and cut in two the bars of iron." There was a tangible weight that was discarded. A weight I had so desperately tried to shed on my own that proved only to be an ineffectual attempt. I needed a hero. O the ebbs and flows we face in our efforts to believe that our heroes, whoever they may be, will not be conquered! On that day, in the black volcanic sand of coastal New Zealand, I came to know that the hero of this story was unconquerable.

What had brought me to the north island of New Zealand was a point in time of my story where I had been given the eyes to see my spiritual orphanhood, but with it, a way out. It had been an ongoing battle, absolutely consumed by self. A fight that pride had plentifully resourced. New Zealand would serve as the start point of finding new language that could appropriately express what it was my spirit had heard in South Africa some months before, on October 2nd, 2014.

When I was living in Cape Town, trying to manage my life with a bewildered list of priorities, I could not get them in order. As a result, I failed to honor my financial responsibilities, and slowly began the rise in pressure that squeezed me out of my home as it was, but also out of the destructive circles that I was moving in. I was not thankful for that. More than ungrateful, I wreaked of bitterness and pride. My hedonistic endeavours seemed only to embolden my arrogance, blinding me with all sorts of counterfeit expressions of comfort, seducing me further into a life of shame and self-rejection. I had been stripped of all that I owned, and with it, any sense of belonging, leaving me only with the impossible thought that I was unlovable and alone.

"I wandered in desert wastes, finding nowhere in the city to dwell in; hungry and thirsty, my soul fainted within me. I was crying out." (Psalm 107: 4-5)

I fast wore out my welcome as I digressed from one couch to the next. It was during this time that I quickly learned why many who were stubbornly homeless preferred it. A quiet place in the reserve, under a tree that would protect you from the elements, seemed a better place to stay from time to time because it never offered the silent pressure of a deadline. It never demanded to know what was next. When you don't have the answers, the questions fast become a burden. You are simply welcome to stay for as long as you can survive. What was simultaneously being worn thin was the energy it demanded to keep this rotting life hidden from my family. Even though the distance between us made it seemingly easier to lie, particularly when offering some manipulative tall story that delivered a request for help in the form of finance, it did not take long, however, to taste the ancient proverb that says getting anything by a lying tongue is but a fleeting vapor, and a snare of death.

"I was a fool through my sinful ways, and because of my iniquities I suffered affliction; I drew near to the gates of death. But then I cried to the Lord in my trouble, and he delivered me from my distress." (Psalm 107:17-19)

I did cry out. And someone heard. As I stood on the street waiting for my brother to arrive, etched into my memory was the look on his face as he compassionately recognized the depths to which I had plummeted. But with not a single hint of condemnation, with his arms wide open, my younger brother embraced me and whispered that it was time to go home. The parable of the prodigal son took place in plain sight on a very ordinary road as I fell into my brother's arms that day.

While this was all unfolding in my life, my brother and his wife were serving at King's Highway Guesthouse, in Somerset West, Cape Town. Here they offered me a small matchbox sized room that would be the reprieve in the storm that my soul longed for. The hardened muck and mire that had glued my eyes shut had slowly started to crack and fall away, yet still, I was blind to the detail and weight of the decision made to "give me a room at the inn." When there is no end in sight, no knowledge of how long ahead of you, only the unknown that is riddled with risk, I have come to learn through my own similar experiences just how challenging that yes can be. But to what lengths would a Father go that His beloved child would find a place to belong! The Advocate had spoken for me. And my brother, his wife, and a precious family of four offered a brave, selfless yes to Christ, my Advocate, that saved my life. I think of Charles Spurgeon's words:

> May the minister be careful to keep the road of faith clear for the seeking sinner, for surely the sinner hath a heavy heart to carry, and we ought to make the road as clear and as smooth as we can. We should make straight paths for the feet of these poor benighted souls. It should be our endeavor to cast loads of promises into every slough that runs across the path, that so it may be a king's highway, and may be safe and easy for travelling for those weary feet that have to carry such a heavy heart.

Jesus said, come to me all who are weary and heavy laden, and He will give us rest, but with sloughs of self-rejection so deep, and paths blocked with rocks of self-hatred, carrying a heart of stone with feet weary from aimless wandering, it seems an awful task to scale these hindrances alone. Faithful are the saints that see through what it is we have done and see us as the loved sons and daughters that we have not yet realized we are.

Grateful for a room now to call my own, as I tended to the garden earning my keep, so too the Great Gardener took me by the hand and walked with me through the garden of my heart. Often in these times, I was graciously accompanied by sweet seven-year-old Amy. She was the youngest of the family that had so lovingly accepted me, but she also was the hands and feet of this Great Gardener, removing from my heart the weeds that strangled the beauty I could no longer see within me. In her innocence and purity, love ministered to my soul with such grace, and kindness, accepting me and affirming my belonging. Amy gave me more than a compliment; she blessed my identity. She was entirely convinced that God loved me. And she knew God as our Father, so that meant I was His son. Amy had no problem telling me this. With her childlike understanding, innocently, she taught me how God speaks, and told me what He thinks of me. Nervously I waited, sure to hear a harsh word from a disappointed, angry Father of whom I was sure that I could not please, but I received only kindness. I remember, as she picked flowers and skipped across the garden, with every step she took, was like the toiling of the soil of my heart, readying me for something soon to come.

On the evening of October 2nd, 2014, the sun had bid us farewell, making way for the moon and her light. I was thinking about how I had seen the sun rise every day for those 33 years of my life. It seemed a simple thought, yet I had a sense that it was summoning me and drawing me toward something greater. As I continued to think, I thought about how darkness had fallen, and how the tides of life had turned so miserably. Looking up at the moon, observing the gentle blanket of light that fell on a resting garden, the thought that provoked me most was that the moonlight would glow until the day returned.

Full of tears, my eyes opened. I looked straight into the pain and into the suffering. I could see how lost I was. I could see the darkness that enshrouded me and what a stumbling fool I had been. But then I saw arriving, like tiny flickering lights in the moonlit sky, the people around me who like beacons of hope cared only to point to the One who saves, bringing a light into my world that I could see what I had been unable to see all my life; that He was there. That the moonlight glowed, waiting for the day to return. He had always been there. "Besides this, you know the time that the hour has come for you to wake from sleep. For salvation is nearer to us now than when we first believed. The night is far gone; the day is at hand. So then let us cast off the works of darkness and put on the armor of light." (Romans 13:11-12)

It quickened me to the thought that my raging heart, after a lifelong fight in the dark, was now the resting garden. I realized, in this unforgettable moment, that the gentle blanket of light had fallen on me. I could not help but surrender.

Our battles feverishly strive on in our refusal to hoist our white flags of surrender because deception says surrender translates to weakness. It has also deceived us enough to believe that weakness has no place in victory. But as we wake up to sonship, the tide turns and our orphaned battles slowly peter out, and with them, the impossible thoughts saying we are alone and cannot be loved are pierced. Perhaps our greatest strength is found in our admission of weakness?

When Jesus uttered upon the cross those words, "It is finished", like a siren it rang throughout the ages, ending the war, paving a way for us to journey on into the heart of the Father. Our surrender acknowledges not our defeat, but His victory that we can take claim in.

Finally, I had run out of strength to hold on, and His strength was made known in my brokenness.

III

From the Inside Out

The potential to arrive at a preferred outcome often offers more ways than one to its destination. Suppose that's one reason why we glean from the stories of others, seeking the treasures that might be found on the pages of their lives. But may we not be too quick to exclude or disqualify stories of fantasy, fairy tale or fiction? Whether fiction or non-fiction, story serves as a powerful manner in which deep-seated ideas are carried to us. Because of the power of story, is that not why fantasy, fairy tale or fiction have the ability to carry truth across in a way that non-fiction sometimes struggles to?   Any good story will lay out for us the classic battle between good and evil, where we see the hero who represents good, and the villain that is the representation of some kind of expression of evil. And hopefully, the hero will prevail, and the villain will be put in his rightful place, where his influence does not triumph. But any great story will put the same battle on display and attempt to lay out for us the fight between good and evil that is simultaneously taking place within the hero, and within the villain, as they come head-to-head and battle out their differences. That grabs our attention! It grips us because we know that is the honest experience of life. The seductive dance of the adulteress with lips so sweet and a speech so smooth calling out to us on the same street corner that Lady Wisdom resides. The tug-of-war for our attention. The back-and-forth between the darkness and the light. The dance we do between spiritual orphanhood and our divine place of belonging. The violent struggle between life and death on this side of the grave. It captivates us. And it does so, because we know we sway from one side to the other but hope deeply that the dark influences of our lives will not ultimately triumph.

We want so desperately the "happily ever after" we find in fairy tales, but we're not too sure what that means in non-fiction and if it's even attainable. Life is not a fairy tale, but it is noteworthy the similarities between fairy tales and our lives. We are all on an adventure, writing out the story of our lives, hoping that our pen steadily moves us toward a happily ever after. However, there seems to me something curious about that. As I come back to those old fairy tales that we once read as kids, with a little more life experience, and hopefully, a little more maturity, it's hard to ignore the thought that comes from this. That there is a possibility of living in our happily ever after today, and need not wait for it to hopefully arrive as the last pages of our lives are turned.

Beauty and the Beast, a well-known fairy tale, one amongst so many, offers an incredible insight to the human heart. There once was a prince, stunning to the eye, but upon opening his mouth, you'd fast recognize the state of this prince's heart; totally selfish and full of arrogance. With no compassion, the pride in this man had led him to mistreat a woman that could not manage the means to the necessities of her life, and so needed to beg for help. As twisted and toxic as begging often gets, it is still a cry for help. This lady in the story happened to be the enchantress in disguise. Because of the way she was treated, she cursed the prince to live out the rest of his life as a repulsive beast until he could learn to love and be loved in return. Is it a reasonable proposition to make that we know something of this curse in our own lives?

When we ignore the nudge to do something good, something seems off. We would do well to pay attention to that. When we decide against acting upon a deceived idea, we have a sense that it was the right thing to do. Subtle as the sense might be, it is present. It is not a simple assignment to find someone that disagrees with that.

"When outsiders who have never heard of God's law follow it more or less by instinct, they confirm its truth by their obedience. They show that God's law is not something alien, imposed on us from without, but woven into the very fabric of our creation. There is something deep within them that echoes God's yes and no, right, and wrong." (Romans 2:14-16)

The twisted prince's actions had led him down a very lonely road. One of the many facets, or fruits, of pride; loneliness. He poorly treated the lowly, and soon to follow was the proverbial fork in the road that offered the chance to choose not just a destination, but also the experience of getting to it. Shame and guilt, another two facets of pride that strangely offer a counterfeit expression of comfort, have a persuasion about them that we subscribe to more often than we would like to admit. And when we do, as he did, we have chosen to be dislocated from the greater body that we are a part of and, of course, the driving force behind all of this is the condemnation that the orphan spirit wants us to dwell in.

Like a harpoon, it lodges itself and lets the line out. Seemingly free for a time to find the limits of the line, everything we do within the confines of this space is insecure and plagued by discomfort. It hinders us until paralyzed and hauls us onto the relentless web of self-rejection. We don't have to go too far or look too deep to find the many voices that partner with the narrative that says we are alone and unlovable. As we wriggle around, struggling to move out from under this condemnation, the trouble is, we know that our actions were not appropriate and so we determine that we deserve our curse and go on in our lives as the hideous beast agreeing with the false report that we are lost and not worth being found.

    Then along comes a headstrong village girl, Belle, in search of her imprisoned father. The prince, corrupted by pride, astonished by Belle's selfless suggestion that he lock her up in exchange for her father's freedom, agrees under the condition she remains in the castle forever. Over time, the hard heart of the prince was being softened by a daughter's selfless love she had not yet for him, but for her father. Merely witnessing that kind of love was managing to address the cold-black-stone in the beast's chest. It was Belle's love, and her willingness to look beyond the prince's appearance, that started to draw the beast out of isolation.

    The once cold-hearted man, who had no time for a beggar woman, was now growing in humility and other favorable attributes. Under the surface, these were the reasons why Belle fell in love with the beast. Not for his outward appearance, but for who she believed he truly was, while still becoming him. That is what true love does. True love refuses to agree with the claims that the orphan spirit relentlessly offers us; that we do not belong. True love, in the spirit of adoption, says that we absolutely belong and need not, or rather, cannot, earn our belonging because it is ours to begin with. True love says there is a room with your name on it, you have the key to it, and no one can take it from you. True love goes as far as saying that you cannot give the key away. You can choose not to use it, but you cannot give it away. The key is yours. "Don't let this rattle you. You trust God, don't you? Trust me. There is plenty of room for you in my Father's home. If that weren't so, would I have told you that I'm on my way to get a room ready for you? And if I'm on my way to get your room ready, I'll come back and get you so you can live where I live. And you already know the road I'm taking." (John 14:1-3) The corrupt prince was living under the spell of the orphan spirit, which, when looked at, appears to be a kind-of-hell this side of the grave. Ironically, he had lost his sense of self as a result of selfishness. Now unattractive and angry at the world, angry at himself, drowning in an ocean of regret, condemned by his own actions and desperately in need of a love that sets free, it seemed he could not save himself. He needed the selfless love of this headstrong village girl. He needed someone who knew that they belonged, and as a result, able to usher in the light into his wicked world so that he could see again.

If I ponder the crucifixion of Christ and how it installs a deep joy and hope in, not just our impeding death, but also our experience of life in getting there, this act so brutal and so fierce, strangely locks-arms with the childlikeness of a fairy tale and says something profound; that there is no place for condemnation on the determined journey of being a loved son or daughter while still becoming it.

"Therefore, there is now no condemnation for those who are in Christ Jesus, because through Christ Jesus the law of the Spirit who gives life has set you free from the law of sin and death." (Romans 8:1-2)

Much like the Beast that became fully human again, beautifully human, we become more like our beautiful King Jesus. And if we are baptized into the death and resurrection of Jesus, then we are also baptized out of spiritual orphanhood and into sonship. We trade in our hearts of stone for malleable hearts of flesh, and it is His Spirit that convinces us of this new way of life as loved sons and daughters.

"And I will give you a new heart, and a new spirit I will put within you. And I will remove the heart of stone from your flesh and give you a heart of flesh. And I will put my Spirit within you and cause you to walk in my statutes and be careful to obey my rules." (Ezekiel 36:26-27)

When we receive this selfless love so great, it changes us from the inside out, and in-turn, we influence the culture around us, and we do it sans anything to prove. Henri Nouwen wrote, "Our humanity comes to its fullest bloom in giving", and that "We become beautiful people when we give whatever we can give: a smile, a handshake, a kiss, an embrace, a word of love, a present, a part of our life, all of our life." Might we even hazard to say that the greatest consummation of our lives lies within giving ourselves to each other.

When we take the risk of believing this thought that is so hostile to the orphan spirit, it gently draws us further into the heart of the Father. The borderless, wide-open space of the Father's heart allows for us to run wildly as we explore the meadows of His love for us. For every thought we pick from the orchard of His heart, as we take in the fragrance of His thoughts for us, we find a settling of the soul that disrupts and threatens anything and everything established in our lives by the orphan spirit. You cannot live in this space without becoming who you have always been. The change is imminent; however, it may not come in an instant. It can happen, but it seems to me the radical moments serve only as a launch pad onto the longer, slower burning roads of the renewal of the mind.

Nonetheless, these narrow, long winding roads that run through the heart of the Father, make for a much smoother and far less insecure experience as we journey and adventure on through life.

IV

Curious Hope

Some great minds have described the intellectual world of addiction as a disaster area. And so, by no means is this an attempt to offer a new intellectual paradigm to consider, I merely want to give context to the statements I make around spiritual orphanhood, sonship, and the observations I've made regards what we think about ourselves, and how crucial it is to discern what, or who, it is informing our thoughts.

In the field that I work, it affords me the privilege and pain of hearing the stories of men and woman as they have experienced them. When asked by friends or family how things are going, and am I enjoying the work that I do, it seems out of place to say that I do, but I do. Of course, I don't take pleasure in the suffering that others experience, but as we bear each other's burdens, so too we share in and celebrate the victories that take place in each other's lives on a daily basis.

"Brothers and sisters, if someone is caught in a sin, you who live by the Spirit should restore that person gently. But watch yourselves, or you also may be tempted. Carry each other's burdens, and in this way, you will fulfill the law of Christ." (Galatians 6:1-2)

The people that I get to spend my time with are searching. And when I ask what it is they are searching for, almost always the first answer that they produce is, themselves. They are looking for the person they are starting to believe they could be. As the conversation continues, at times for months long, and the troubled waters start to settle down, I'll ask the same question. And now, with the discovery of self that has somewhat floated to the surface, it brings with it the desire to know one's purpose. As the conversations forge forward that circle around finding meaning, purpose, and identity, there is time spent evaluating what is being focused on in the search for purpose because what we behold, gives great clues to why certain things look the way that they do.

Jesus is knocking on the doors of men and woman with the hopes that they would answer and let Him in. At times they do, allowing Him to take front-and-centre upon whom they now set their sights. This gaze draws them up and into the heart of the Father. And as the Spirit assures them of their divine place of belonging, in time, a person that was once so enshrouded by darkness now moves into the light. It is no longer a spiritual orphan using the tools of recovery, but a loved son or daughter abiding in Jesus. And that tends to bear good, long-lasting fruit with sobriety, or a life-well-lived, being a symptom of an abiding life.

With the opioid crisis ravaging lives and taking them at a staggering rate, which seems only to climb from year to year, being this close to it has demanded from me an evaluation of my abiding life, and what it is that I behold. I think of how a body of water in front of a stunning mountain scape, to some extent, beholds it. As I observe the reflection of the backdrop of the pond on the water that holds it, I fondly remember that the best reflections that I have ever seen have been on still waters. What am I beholding, and am I like still waters, seemed an appropriate question in my evaluation. Serving in an environment that has no room for shortcuts or quick fixes has also called me to pause for a consideration of my own pace, and to examine to what degree I allow others to know me as I endeavor to get to know them. In this, as we do the work to get to know ourselves much better, it is incredible that God so desires to reveal Himself as our Father, through Jesus, and in that exposing our true, God-given identities. Not as quickly as I would like to admit, I have finally learnt that I am found in Him. I am now much less interested in asking who am I, instead I ask, who are You, God?

It seems to me that our identities inform the way we approach the plans and purposes of our lives, and not the other way around. So, the question is, what, or who, is informing our identities? Contingent on the clarity that one has on their identity is the pace they walk with through the course of their days. But if identity is threatened, things get uncomfortable, and the orphan spirit offers a counterfeit expression of comfort and attempts to lure a person into a false sense of being and belonging.

By observation, it seems to me that what is being searched for is not at all exclusive to the citizens of the dark underworld of excessive drug and alcohol use; it is us all who have been, or are, in search of the same thing; true identity that is found in our divine place of belonging.

When both are challenged and we do not know yet where to run, because of the horror stories that we have endured, counterfeit expressions of comfort are our go-to, because it seems inconceivable to be called a loved son or daughter with such a lofty thing as that of a divine place of belonging. It seems even when we have found our way, and the sun of sonship has risen on our dark night, it is at times not that obvious to us that we can run into the arms of the Father when crisis impinges on us.

When we are in despair, we are tempted to go back to our tombs, our old orphan ways, the place of the dead, in search of the way out into life, like Mary of Magdalene did looking for Jesus.

"While they were wondering about this, suddenly two men in clothes that gleamed like lightning stood beside them. In their fright the women bowed down with their faces to the ground, but the men said to them, 'Why do you look for the living among the dead? He is not here; he has risen! Remember how he told you, while he was still with you in Galilee: The Son of Man must be delivered over to the hands of sinners, be crucified and on the third day be raised again.' Then they remembered his words." (Luke 24:4-8)

Christ's victory was final, and we have been invited to step into, and live from, His victory. But what appears to be a very necessary practice in the life of a believer is the endeavor of learning to win quicker by reminding ourselves, and each other, of His victory. Whether the writers who penned the Gospels, and particularly this account of when Mary "went looking for the living among the dead" intended for us to consider it this way, I find it a brilliant example of what we do when our identities are being challenged. We look for the living among the dead, not remembering His words about being raised from the dead and forget that we too have walked out of the tomb when we identify with the life of Christ. We forget Paul's instruction to identify only with the life of Christ, not with our old ways. And if we are identifying with the life of Christ, we are identifying with the truth that we are loved sons and daughters of whom the Father is well-pleased.

"But now that faith has come, we are no longer under a guardian, for in Christ Jesus you are all sons of God, through faith. For as many of you as were baptized into Christ have put on Christ." (Galatians 3:25-27)

It is absolutely critical that we find ourselves at the foot of the cross, gazing into the blinding light of the crucifixion, and allowing it to wash over us with the love of the Father we so desperately need. But we must also move on from the cross. It is right, when necessary, to "walk" the orphan spirit back to the cross and remember that Jesus drank from this cup to reconcile us back to the Father. But then, with Christ, we must walk away from the cross! And in the same way that Jesus was anointed and then wrapped in linen, would we allow Him to anoint us with the spirit of adoption, and wrap us with His love, giving us the ability to walk out of the tomb leaving behind the orphan hanging on the cross.

Should you examine the Psalms, you recognize that collectively, the authors have masterfully crafted a songbook for the soul as it swings between coming back to the cross and walking out of the tomb. Divided into five books, each with a very clear posture of heart, when held up altogether, they stunningly, and unashamedly, reveal not only God's immaculate character, but a very real depiction of the rollercoaster ride our minds are often on. On occasion, I have thought out loud, wondering if the collective expression of our life experiences is not better understood when examined the same way? Curiously, the question has offered hope.

The final Psalms of the fifth book ends with five consecutive "hallelujahs" that invite us to join in the beautiful crescendo of worship across all creation. But I implore you to notice the stark contrast to that of the opening psalms which, although they contain periodic moments of hope, are mostly written from a place of lamentation, distress, and even doubt in God's justice. It seems because the scales tip so drastically from one side to the other, much like life, there is something in it that a person in peril wants to grab a hold of.

Found here is a glimmer of hope, that perchance, like the Psalms, our endeavors have the potential to come together to reveal God's immaculate character, ultimately hailing from our lives the hallelujahs He intended to hear from us from the beginning.

It is astounding how far a glimmer of hope can carry a man.

V

Well-Informed

If from our lives there hails a hallelujah, or we are found in despair looking through the lens of lamentation, by now, we know that the manner in which we handle these respectively, is greatly influenced by what it is we believe about God, and ourselves. A simpler way of painting that picture is, how do you handle your victories and losses? Perhaps the question is better answered by someone you can trust to speak the truth in love. To note, I am not suggesting that if you are in a season of lament, that you are losing. By no means. But for the sake of explanation, I offer for your consideration—we would do well in learning how to win and lose with honor. No one enjoys the loser that takes no responsibility, casts blame to all other team members, and elevates themselves above all others while throwing a tantrum. And neither do we enjoy the arrogant winner that flaunts his victory, and pompously parades around as if our entire existence depended on the victory. A loved son or daughter knows that their victory, or loss, will not jeopardize their place in the home and so, are able to celebrate their victories well, and acknowledge their losses with honor. No victory comes with the reward of more love from the Father.

Conversely, no loss has the power to move you out from under His umbrella of love. We are safe!

"But God, being rich in mercy, because of the great love with which he loved us, even when we were dead in our trespasses, made us alive together with Christ–by grace you have been saved–and raised us up with him and seated us with him in the heavenly places in Christ Jesus, so that in the coming ages he might show the immeasurable riches of his grace in kindness toward us in Christ Jesus." (Ephesians 2:4-7)

With whatever it is that you put your hands to, who is it that is doing the works? Is it the insecure, lost soul wandering around in spiritual orphanhood, striving to climb his or her way up and into the heavenly place of belonging? Or is it the loved son or daughter that knows there can be no result that would possibly sway the love that the Father has for them because, it was by grace that they have been given life, raised up, and seated in their divine place of belonging?

With an identity built upon the rock, it makes possible to hail the hallelujah, or to cry the honest lament, without being swept up and away by either of the two. Loved sons and daughters, with a deep conviction of their divine place of belonging, are not swayed by the accusations of the deceiver that constantly try to disjoint them in the communities to which they belong. I am of the persuasion that it is crucial to pay attention to this because we do life within the context of community, and how we carry ourselves and relate to each other within it makes a difference to the overall health of the community.

"Rather, speaking the truth in love, we are to grow up in every way into him who is the head, into Christ, from whom the whole body, joined and held together by every joint with which it is equipped, when each part is working properly, makes the body grow so that it builds itself up in love." (Ephesians 4:15-16)

At this juncture, I must confess that the thoughts that follow have been difficult to offer out loud.

I describe spirituality as the aspect of humanity that refers to how we as individuals seek and express meaning and purpose, and our ability to factor these aspects into our lives with others. With that, it is the way we experience our connectedness to the moment, to self, to others, to nature and to the significant or sacred. Might we hazard to say it is the very difference between life and death this side of the grave, because it has the ability to nudge us toward the latter in the worst way if it is unwell. It is what gives us the means to find meaning and purpose, and certainly then, curates the way we express what we believe inwardly, in an appropriate manner, outwardly.

This is more often than not done within the context of behaviours, values, rules for conduct, perhaps rituals that are associated with religious tradition or even denomination. So, the question is, how would you diagnose your spirituality – to answer broadly, is it well, or unwell? More importantly, what is funding your spirituality? Is it the orphan spirit, or has the spirit of adoption been given the space to pursued you that you are undeniably a loved son or daughter and as a result, you carry within you an inner set of beliefs that have not been debauched by insecurity?

But what about religion? What role does religion play with regards our inner set of beliefs that I believe seek, because they need, an appropriate outward expression in line with our God-given desires of the heart? Is what we are doing lining up with what it is that we believe? Here in North America, it seems to me the word religion is as good as a swear word. Particularly in the church. It has become the popular narrative to hold one fist up to religion and in the other, flying the flag of "relationship" yet still beckoning a person to join their services on a Sunday. And if they are more the progressive type, they may say something to the likes of, "The church is not a building, people are the church", and then encourage you to maintain some kind of community, centered around what it is that you and your community believe, and practice it. That is in basic terms, the very definition of religion. Do they not mean the religious spirit? When looking into it, yes.

What some have meant is that they hold no place for the religious spirit. Sadly, there are many that have turned their backs on religion simply because they don't understand the difference between the two.

It is as a result of oppressive and controlling expressions of religion funded by the orphan spirit, that there has been a deep hurt, and finally, a resentment toward any kind of religion, and anyone that makes any such claim about being a part of it must be a tyrant. And it is typically at this point that a person might walk away and say something like, "I'm not into religion, I'm spiritual." The problem with this is we need it. We orient our lives to that which we believe, and a healthy expression of religion that is congruent with these beliefs gives us a necessary balance, a sense of purpose, and at least the opportunity to connect with others that believe the same thing.

An applaudable rebuttal might be that Jesus never came to install religion. I agree. Leonard Ravenhill said this, "Jesus did not come into the world to make bad men good. He came into the world to make dead men live!" But once living, we seek to connect with others and practice what it is that we believe collectively. Worshiping together. Praying together. Baptism. Sermon. Fasting and feasting. Communion!

"And he took bread, and when he had given thanks, he broke it and gave it to them, saying, 'This is my body, which is given for you. Do this in remembrance of me.'" (Luke 22:19)

With ritual, Jesus encouraged us to remember Him. Perhaps Jesus' point was not religion, but healthy living in union with Him. But when we unpack what healthy living looks like, particularly through the lens of Christ, it seems to me to be healthy connection with Him and others. And a healthy expression of what it is that we believe tends to serve those relationships in a deep and rich way.

So I offer a thought–instead of turning our nose up to religion too quickly, might we ask the same questions we did with regards to our spirituality; how would you diagnose the connection between the means you have to express your inner beliefs, to what it is you believe? To answer broadly, is it well, or unwell? But more importantly, what informs this relationship? Is it the orphan spirit, or has the spirit of adoption been given the space to pursued you that you are undeniably a loved son or daughter and as a result, you carry within you an inner set of beliefs that have not been debauched by insecurity, and now with it, a community of like-minded folk who practise with you what it is you believe?

To say it differently, a well-informed religion that is being facilitated by a loved son or daughter, does not bring with it a heavy-handed, works based effort to find love from the Father, it brings with it a space to practise what it is that we believe, and a chance to express a love that is already ours, collectively, to God and each other.

Both our religion and our spirituality integrate us as people into this experience we know as being alive. But without a solid spiritual foundation sustained best in a healthy community, which often includes some kind of religious expression that is congruent (hopefully) with what the community believes, even our best-intentioned endeavors of living well, will be found under attack by the lies and self-appointed powers of deception that the orphan spirit offers. When our spirituality and the means to express it are unwell, we are susceptible to being disconnected and potentially led to being isolated from one another.

There is a temporal relief, and a sort of bliss, that comes from being disconnected from oneself and others when we are constantly battling the dark chaos within. This darkness is also known otherwise as "spiritual bankruptcy." A phrase apparently well-known amongst the recovery communities around the world. I prefer the term spiritual orphanhood.

In this darkness, what pulls us out into the light is love. A love that has us daring to believe that we are in fact not alone, capable of being loved and loving others, accepted, even as we are, and that our broken hearts have this strange ability to lead us into blessing. This love convinces us that we are sons and daughters of the Most High and that we have a divine place of belonging.

"The Lord is near to the broken-hearted and saves the crushed in spirit." (Psalm 34:18)

This is uncharted territory for so many, but it offers help by producing a further few questions – have you been deceived into believing something about God and yourself that has led you down a hopeless road of despair and isolation? Has the orphan spirit challenged your divine place of belonging and convinced you, falsely, of your worthlessness? What have you subscribed to that does not lineup with the heart of a loving Father and His thoughts about you, His child?

I have observed that in the process of facing our fears, it is helpful to be reminded of our belonging and acceptance. It helps guide us to find a treasure so precious that stirs in us a deep joy even in the suffering. I have noticed that we find meaning and purpose as we adopt the responsibility of facing our pain, and not turning from it, which affords us the honor of passing on the sacred pages of our stories like a blazing torch from one generation to the next because it offers hope, wisdom, and the prospect of an adopted life well-lived.

There is much to learn, but this I do know, the orphan spirit, is no match to that of the heart of the Father. We are loved, but we need to be reminded of that frequently.

VI

Wisdom Has Her Reasons

As the day dawned and the sun spilled over the sandstone rooftops of Jerusalem, a dark tragic event was as well coming to light. A lady of the night lay bare on her bed with babe at breast, slowly waking to tend to her motherly duties. Something was wrong, though. The infant lay eerily still. Her eyes were unable to focus as she scanned for signs of life in the darkroom. Her heart sank. The child was dead.

But as the morning light crept further into the harlot's room and onto this grave unfolding, she shockingly realized that this dead child was not her child! She had given birth three days before her housemate gave birth to a babe of her own – the babe who lay dead in her arms. Frantically, she searched her out only to find betrayal. What she had walked into was her babe being nursed by a foreign breast. There was no one else around. No eye witnesses. Just the full persuasion of the connection a mother has with her child with nothing to prove it but her word.

A mother had smothered her baby by mistake, and traded the corpse for another mother's child, thinking that she would get away with it.

The two ladies, that were prostitutes, took the living child and made their way to the king of the region to settle the grim dispute. The dialogue commenced, one woman making her case explaining to the king that she, and the woman with her, had both given birth to a child, one three days after the other, and that they both live under the same roof. She continued to lay out the details for the king, explaining that the child had been smothered while he was sleeping, and the mother of the dead child being blinded by pain must have made the heinous exchange while she, too, was sleeping.

And so began the chaotic debacle of one word against another's for a child whose place of belonging was being challenged. It is stunning to consider that this infant boy might represent us, and that the corrupt harlot represents all that the world has to offer in a bid to "steal" us from our divine place of belonging.

Menacingly, that dark night in Jerusalem has happened repeatedly throughout the generations. Sons and daughters, caught in the middle of the chaotic debacle that takes place in their minds of whether or not they are loved and accepted for who they truly are, which leaves them unsure of where it is that they belong.

In the same way that the king of the region gave ear to the issue, so too do we need the King of kings to intervene for us today as our place of belonging and our identities are being challenged. The author of this story labored the beauty and fruits of wisdom. Just how Godly wisdom found a way to disarm the chaos of the situation, find out the truth, and do justice without having been at the scene of this dismal crime. But there is much more in this story to look at.

Out loud, the king offered a question that perhaps those who were in the room might have been thinking, "What shall we do!?" But all that did was catapult the woman into a fruitless fighting frenzy yet again. A moment had passed before the king requested his servants bring him his sword.

The king's servants complied and brought the sword, and if we can allow for imagination to have its way, I suppose they brought with them not just the sword, but also a tension with questions that needed answers. For what does the king need a sword!? What will he do with it!? What is the king thinking!?

Preposterously, the king commanded, "Cut the living baby in two. Give half to one and a half to the other." It was at this point that the story took another ominous turn. Emotions got the better of the actual mother. She broke down. She gave up her just and right desires of wanting her child back. And for the sake of her child's life, with love she cried, "Oh no, master! Give her the whole baby alive. Don't kill him!" Sinisterly, the corrupt prostitute succumbs to the evil tug from the depths of darkness yet again and says, "If I can't have him, you can't have him. Cut away!" The discerning king that he was gave a decision; "Give the living baby to the first woman. Nobody is going to kill this baby. She is the actual mother."

"All this is from God, who through Christ reconciled us to himself and gave us the ministry of reconciliation; that is, in Christ, God was reconciling the world to himself, not counting their trespasses against them, and entrusting to us the message of reconciliation." (2 Corinthians 5:18-20)

The king's way with his sword had reconciled the child to his loving mother. Similarly, the King of kings has reconciled us to our loving Father, and His sword, that is His Spirit, bears witness with our spirit that we are children of God, severing the connection to the orphan spirit.

"The Spirit himself bears witness with our spirit that we are children of God, and if children, then heirs—heirs of God and fellow heirs with Christ, provided we suffer with him in order that we may also be glorified with him." (Romans 8:16-18)

That dark night, a child's life was lost, and another was threatened. It is a stunning parallel from the king and his sword that delivered a child back into his rightful place of belonging, to that of King Jesus and His Spirit, that reconciled us to the Father, our divine place of belonging and gives us His Spirit in our aid to believe it. But with the multi-faceted unfolding that this story carries with it, we wonder, had the king been under the influence of the orphan spirit himself, insecure and unsure, unable to decide what to do in this terrible moment because of the fear of man, would the infant boy have found his way back into his mother's arms?

The results of a man secure in his Father's love was that he could think clearly. He could think through the absurd solution that he offered, knowing that God's wisdom is from above, it is pure, then peaceable, it is gentle, and easy to be intreated, it is full of mercy and good fruits, without partiality, and without hypocrisy. King Solomon knew that God's wisdom delivers justice. God's wisdom has a reason that is ever so dear to the heart of God; that a displaced child would find his or her way back into a safe place of belonging.

This true-life drama has masterfully threaded together some thoughts for our consideration. We can see how far selfish ambition is willing to go. We see on display the sacrifice that love was willing to make for the sake of another. Stunningly documented was a man's willingness to act upon what Lady Wisdom had offered him. No matter how ludicrous it may have appeared in the moment, he had the courage and wherewithal to move forward, which subtly hints to us that there can be no room for insecurity. This speaks to an intimacy with the source of wisdom, trusting that it disarms chaos and brings justice, but also gives us the quiet confidence we need when walking through the storms of spiritual orphanhood.

When the insecure are at the helm, it will be a tough storm to fare. The captain needs the trust of his crew who look to him for leadership because it is the captain who needs to make tough decisions for the safety of his fellow seafarers. When the winds are raging and the waves come crashing in, one glance over to a confident and secure captain has the ability to calm the crew enough that they may continue on with their tasks. But should they turn to skipper only to find a man that is grappling not with the matter at hand, but consumed by the fear of man, consumed by self, their trust will cut and run, causing fear and confusion. Should the skipper in his insecurity have nowhere to turn, the only option will be to those around him. Casting blame, unrealistic expectations, assumptions, and excuses. These are the fruits of an insecure soul unwilling to take responsibility, making the high claim that they have everyone else's best interests in mind. When the insecure are at the helm, it tends to be a tyrannical expression of leadership which causes fear and confusion and ultimately, resentment toward leadership itself.

But when all Israel heard of the judgment that this king had rendered, they stood in awe of the king, because they perceived that the wisdom of God was in him to do justice. These are the fruits of a man that believes the things that God says about him.

The fruits of a leader who knows who he is, is life. In the instance of this story, a child found his rightful place back in the arms of his loving mother.

Our insecurities have disabled us terribly, hindering us from living in the fullness of love and all the benefits therein. But our insecurities can also serve as a helpful indicator. Where you see insecurity, bless. Partner with the spirit of adoption and bless from the Father's heart the truth of their acceptance and belonging. Like the fight for that infant boy's place of belonging, and how the king and his sword implemented a just decision, so too the King of kings has done what He said He would do; reconciled us to the Father. And that is our message. Reconciliation.

Let us turn the inner ear of our hearts toward the quiet call of The Counsellor and remind each other that the King of kings has delivered justice. Let us remind each other of our acceptance and divine place of belonging. Let us continue to tell these stories of harlots, kings, and displaced children that find their way home because Godly wisdom will accept nothing less. Let us faithfully remind each other that it is wisdom that comes by fearing the Lord first, that will see us fare-well in these trying times of identity theft that we are in.

"A wise man is full of strength, and a man of knowledge enhances his might, for by wise guidance you can wage your war, and in abundance of counselors there is victory." (Proverbs 24:5-8)

Wisdom is what enables us to deal honorably with the tragedies of life. Life is full of crisis. There is no escaping that. However, we can find a way to navigate crisis appropriately so that we don't shipwreck our lives further. When living in the fear of the Lord, we have every opportunity to leave a legacy that others can step into and carry on for the next. In spite of the difficulties, wisdom would give us the ability to be salt and light for others when dark times are upon them.

I had spent some treasured time in the Middle East, about 200 kilometers east of the same sandstone roofs under which this dramatic story unfolded. Stationed in a small town called Al Mafraq in Jordan, we would serve the victims of a war that had been ongoing for several years prior. Certainly, dark times were upon these people. Your finger did not need to be on the pulse for too long before being struck by the reality that mere smarts were not going to bear much fruit. We needed to move in the fear of the Lord, so that it equipped us with wisdom. The same wisdom that delivered justice for the mother and carried a child back into his rightful place of belonging.

"You are the salt of the earth. But if the salt loses its saltiness, how can it be made salty again? It is no longer good for anything, except to be thrown out and trampled underfoot. You are the light of the world. A town built on a hill cannot be hidden. Neither do people light a lamp and put it under a bowl. Instead, they put it on its stand, and it gives light to everyone in the house. In the same way, let your light shine before others, that they may see your good deeds and glorify your Father in heaven." (Matthew 5:13-16)

Salt flavors food and is used as a binder and stabilizer. It is also a food preservative, as bacteria cannot thrive in the presence of a high amount of salt. While the methods have advanced, salt was also used to rub on the wick of candles because it would prolong the burning of the wick, and with that, the candle would burn much brighter. Wisdom is like salt. Wisdom will preserve the good that we have going for us. Wisdom will bring out the good that is hidden among us. Wisdom will sustain us and have us burn brighter than what we once did before, being a lamp on a hill that illuminates the hope that others struggle to see.

Godly wisdom does indeed have a reason; that a displaced child, lost in the dark, would find his or her rightful place back in the arms of the Father, because in that, He is glorified!

PART II
THE WEFT

DIVINE PLACE OF BELONGING

VII

Sealing the End of Our Braided Lines

Trying to make sense of the thread that has been weaved so far has me thinking of Corrie ten Boom's famous tapestry quote. Of course, not entirely regardless of the atrocities that Corrie had endured, because, understandably, the sorrow that she had experienced is what makes her quote so powerful. I highlight it more for the imagery of weaving together seemingly inharmonious events that, in the end, do achieve a coherent thought.

"My Life is but a weaving between my Lord and me; I cannot choose the colors He worketh steadily. Oft times He weaveth sorrow and I, in foolish pride, forget He sees the upper, and I the underside. Not till the loom is silent and the shuttles cease to fly, shall God unroll the canvas and explain the reason why."

I have lightly mulled over the proverbial forks in the road that we journey on – those that beg from us a choice – pride or humility. And I have apportioned some pages to that of our thought life, and who, or perchance for some, what it might be that informs it. I have skimmed on the power of story, and sparingly offered insight to wisdom and her reasons, but as if the warp and weft make true a mess from the underside, the hope is as I turn to the upper side, that the loom of this book would reveal an image that bears witness to love, sonship, and our divine place of belonging as the loom of your life has not yet been silenced. It is the golden thread woven from the start to the coming conclusion. In this effort to make complex ideas sound almost elementary, as the forthcoming pages are turned, faith filled, I hope that the spirit of adoption would seal the end of the braided lines of spiritual orphanhood in our lives.

"…even as he chose us in him before the foundation of the world, that we should be holy and blameless before him. In love he predestined us for adoption to himself as sons through Jesus Christ, according to the purpose of his will, to the praise of his glorious grace, with which he has blessed us in the Beloved." (Ephesians 1:4-6)

He chose us. In love, He foreordained us as sons and daughters to Himself through what Christ accomplished and commissioned His Spirit to convince us of that. But we are not easily convinced, and it is not so obvious to us why that might be true when we know all too well what kinds of lives we have lived. Certainly not lives that we feel could, or even should, be attached to words like holy, or blameless, and as a result, we turn, no, we run, the other way to "save face." When we do this, we seize to believe that we might see God in ourselves, and in others. Perhaps that is why it can be so painful when staring into the mirror. "Who am I!?", "Surely no good thing can be found in this reflection of a stranger", "Worthless", "Lost", "Too far-gone", fill in your blank. When we look the other way, insecurity floods in and pushes us toward the darkness where our true identities are displaced. Here, all sorts of counterfeit expressions of comfort beckon, offering up a residency in spiritual orphanhood. A false sense of belonging, putting pause on our becoming of what we have always been; a loved and accepted son or daughter with a divine place of belonging in the Father's heart.

I have said nothing new. Nothing especially progressive. There are thousands of books written that echo the age-old message of love and sonship, and there needs to be a thousand more. But as I think about the possibility of love, something that Jesus said offers itself as a doorway to divine discovery.

"My command is this: Love each other as I have loved you. Greater love has no one than this: to lay down one's life for one's friends. You are my friends if you do what I command. I no longer call you servants because a servant does not know his master's business. Instead, I have called you friends, for everything that I learned from my Father I have made known to you." (John 15:10-15)

No greater love than to lay our lives down for another, understanding that it is this love relationship between the Father and Son that first informs our love, and then governs the way in which we express it as sons and daughters. I hazard a proposition, not in challenging what John the Beloved has written, but to preface it. Perhaps the greatest way we might love God, so that we might love others, is to let God love us?

"God is love. When we take up permanent residence in a life of love, we live in God and God lives in us. This way, love has the run of the house, becomes at home, and mature in us, so that we're free of worry on Judgment Day—our standing in the world is identical with Christ's. There is no room in love for fear. Well-formed love banishes fear. Since fear is crippling, a fearful life—fear of death, fear of judgment—is one not yet fully formed in love.

We, though, are going to love—love and be loved. First we were loved, now we love. He loved us first." (1 John 4:16-20)

Putting this kind of love into practice, that is, allowing ourselves to be loved, brings with it an invitation to be known. To be truly known. As people, we are desperate to be seen, but it seems we are too scared to be known. How far are we willing to let others in and know us, allowing for the love that has bloomed to blossom? How we answer this question is almost certainly contingent to the degree on which we "let God love us", and trust that He will be with us in our vulnerability as we do it with others!

I have learnt much since these thoughts first captivated me. I have observed in myself first, and then in those that are around me in the work that I do, that letting someone love us can be especially difficult when we turn away from the trauma that we have endured either at the end of our own hand, or someone else's. My assignment at this time, as I pen these pages, is to wade through the lies and deception that have managed to convince a person falsely of their spiritual orphanhood, and to expose them. That is putting it especially lightly, but there is no sense to labor the rotten fruit of the orphan spirit and the specific dark details that have reigned on for too long, at times, resulting in death. Instead, a far more fruitful benefaction is to share the observations made when courageous men and woman move beyond the boundaries of bitterness that set in when they feel unseen. Because it is here, beyond these boundaries, where the adventure of sanctification awaits!

I know in my own life, I overcame the fear I found in the risk of letting others know me, truly know me, when I laid down the desire to be seen, and acknowledged that my standing in the world is identical with Christ's. This acknowledgment has moved me from going as far as dancing on the fringe of believing that I have nothing to prove, where I had been plagued by discomfort and insecurity, to being comfortable in my skin, and able to discern the difference between invitation and temptation. It seems to me we are drawn into invitation, but with temptation, it is different. With temptation, the events tend to come armed with compulsion.

The invitation is to believe that you have always been a loved child with a divine place of belonging. And the temptation is to believe that you need first to become a loved child, and then to earn your way into your divine place of belonging.

This has been true for so many others. If we are identical to Christ, the Father looks at us as heirs with Christ His Son and sees in us as well a beloved son or daughter. This has moved me into the wide-open space of a settled spirit. I am funded now by a love so deep that helps me greatly to open up and be known by others. Known as I am, and for who I am becoming, without anything to prove. The lies are not necessarily silenced, but I now have the ears to hear otherwise, that I may choose otherwise.

"My dear children, let's not just talk about love; let's practice real love. This is the only way we'll know we're living truly, living in God's reality. It's also the way to shut down debilitating self-criticism, even when there is something to it. For God is greater than our worried hearts and knows more about us than we do ourselves." (1 John 3:18-20)

I am learning not to follow my heart, instead I follow Jesus, because He is the healer and far greater than my worried heart. And when I follow Jesus, He walks with me into the arms of the Father where I belong.

DIVINE PLACE OF BELONGING

VIII

But Would You?

The Good Samaritan has on many occasions shown compassion on me, bound up my wounds, and found for me a place in the inn where I would find restoration. When I think of these moments in life, it seems beyond the bounds of possibility that I would walk away from these saving occasions as the nine lepers did: without gratitude. It has always been easier to identify with the one leper, who upon realizing that Jesus had healed him, could not go on, and needed to return and throw himself at the feet of Jesus to express his gratitude. While these happenings in my life resource me with great reason for gratitude, they also beckon me beyond just the gift. It tilts my chin up, shifting my focus from His hands, and onto His face. It draws me in and helps me to press on beyond rejoicing with great joy because I have found evidence of His presence, and into a state of worship, as I enter into in His presence.

"When they saw the star, they rejoiced exceedingly with great joy. And going into the house, they saw the child with Mary his mother, and they fell down and worshiped him." (Matthew 2:10-11)

It summons me toward my place of belonging, that is, with the Giver of the gift.

Thankfully, the love of God does not seize to exist in our inability to be grateful for it. But important to note, neither will any act of service conjure from the Father more of His love for us. He loves us completely. It is we who, when strengthened by the indwelling of Christ in our hearts, like a blossoming flower garden, we slowly open until we are in the full bloom of His love.

"So that Christ may dwell in your hearts through faith–that you, being rooted and grounded in love, may have strength to comprehend with all the saints what is the breadth and length and height and depth, and to know the love of Christ that surpasses knowledge, that you may be filled with all the fullness of God." (Ephesian 3:17-19)

When we willingly let His love in, we begin to orient our lives toward this love, which slowly starts tending to our spiritual orphanhood, coaxing us into sonship. He gave Himself to us that we would be reconciled to the Father. We love God, and others, because He loved us first. And this orientation delivers with it a desire to fulfill the former for the rest of our lives.

"And you shall love the Lord your God with all your heart and with all your soul and with all your mind and with all your strength.' The second is this: 'You shall love your neighbor as yourself.' There is no other commandment greater than these.'" (Mark 12:30-31)

Upon offering the story of the good Samaritan to a listener, and with it, the question of who they identify with most in the story, more often than not, nobly the answer is the good Samaritan, with little regard to the confession of being "the man that fell amongst the robbers."

However, before being able to sustain being the good Samaritan, I believe it to be incredibly helpful if we first acknowledge our dire need for The Good Samaritan, Jesus. In loving others, what a difference it makes when we concede that we have been loved first. When we do, our acts of service take on a fragrance that is inviting and leads to life. If you could bottle this fragrance, label it, and put it on the shelf, it would be called "Sonship." But this fragrance does not work that way, and neither does such a treasure of incalculable value belong on the shelf. It is not but a mere "spraying on" of sonship—the fragrance is Christ, that carries with Him the spirit of adoption that changes us from the inside out. He came to transfigure our thinking from spiritual orphanhood to that of loved sons and daughters, because He came to reconcile us to the Father.

I have always been a loved son. But I have not always believed that. My transfiguration from spiritual orphanhood into sonship has been a slow road to glory. Every provision I have received, every "parting of the sea", or "mountain moved", every pearl of wisdom, every bit of kindness, every good gift that I have received from the Good Giver, I am of the persuasion that all of it is intended to convince me of this, that I am not alone, I am loved, I am a son, and with that, I have a heavenly room in my Father's house. More than that; that I am in union with the Father. Being assured of this removes from the thrones of our lives the fear of man to which we have bowed a knee. This makes way for the King to take up His rightful position – as Lord. The One who reconciled us to the Father, making this union possible.

    He ushers us into a place where the tender touch of the Father would gently tear down the bogus supports of spiritual orphanhood that have been our foundation. But unlike the brute force of a demolition crew, the Holy Spirit brilliantly props us up as He re-installs the substructure of sonship with His unconditional love. We are so loved by the Father that while we were at our worst, He sent His Beloved Son Jesus to reconcile us back to Him. Too many to count are the quiet, loving nudges to sonship. A pivotal moment in my life had taught me in the most spectacularly challenging way that He loves me the same, no matter what it is that I do or don't do. And from this place, this place of belonging, has been my launchpad for obedience, where I have found my transformation.

We don't obey because we must. We obey because we want to. And it is imperative that we do because it is in our followership of Jesus that we are transformed. It is not duty, it is delight. God's love does transform us, but it seems only if we let it. If it were not so, the world that we live in would be an extraordinarily different place. It would also be a world without choice. And should we extract from the world, choice, then there can be no love. Love cannot exist without the possibility of choice.

As I offer a short story that puts on display this love, I hope to offer by way of the story that just because you have found it an impossibility to be called a loved son or daughter with a divine place of belonging, it does not nullify the truth of it. And should you turn your eyes to the horizon of sonship, the relentless love of the Father will deeply challenge your spiritual orphanhood.

"I came for the sick…" These were the words that echoed deep within me as I exited the small town of Riviersonderend, en route Jeffreys Bay in the Eastern Cape of South Africa. I was on my way home from Cape Town after visiting family when in my peripherals, too quick to be sure, up from the bush beside the road waved a man's arm that had on it a small band-aid. Was someone calling for help!? I wondered. Then again, "I came for the sick", "I came for the sick." It would not let me go. Almost involuntarily, the utterance from within me that spilled out from my lips—"Yes, Lord." I made a U-turn and headed back.

I took my best guess and parked where I thought I saw this peculiar picture and said again under my breath, "Yes, Lord." I stepped out into the inescapable heat, and after a few unsettled steps, there he was. Unable to speak, burnt terribly from the sun, all that this man had to offer as a clue to his story was an illegible doctor's note, and a small piece of cotton wool plastered down onto his forearm with a band-aid. The one seemed to confirm the other, however, never shed any light and brought with it only a sense of urgency. He was also missing a shoe.

Having nothing with me, we headed back into town to find some water and perhaps something to eat. We would see about that. After some time having gone by, he mustered up enough energy to say thank you, although unnecessary, and to give me a third clue as to his story. That was more necessary. He wanted to get to a small settlement, presumably home, in Still Bay, which was roughly two hours away from where we were. It turned out we were both going in that direction, so we traveled together.

He gasped for air! Utterly confused, he demanded to know where we were! We had only been travelling for 45 minutes, leaving us with a little over an hour to go. This gave him enough time to find his bearings and to rattle my world by letting me into his. This man had been raped in prison. What landed him there was theft. He lost his wife, and with her, his eight-year-old daughter, because the burden of living with a criminal whose body was shutting down from HIV/AIDS contracted from the rape was too much to bear. He also had a type of epilepsy that had not been specifically diagnosed, he just knew that periodically he fell into seizure. He had never met his father, and his mother abandoned him. He was an orphan. Spiritually as well. He was absolutely alone – as far as he was concerned.

With no recollection of how he got to the dry ditch where I had found him, it quite surprised me that he had managed to navigate us to his home. When we got there, it became evident to me that he was no longer welcome. How these people aggressively made that known to him led me to believe they may have had something to do with the doctor's note and the black and blue rib cage he wore. I wondered if they had put him in hospital. This was an extremely hostile situation, and we needed to flee. So we did.

My home was a little over four hours away, give or take. It seemed almost a cruel thing to ask because I had a sense that I knew the answer already, but I had nothing else in the moment. Carelessly, I asked what he thought was next. The silence was painful. He hadn't seen his mother in decades since she had abandoned him, yet he suspected that his mother lived somewhere in a city called Gqeberha (Port Elizabeth) and decided he might try to find her there. Strangely, Port Elizabeth was the next major stop, another hour up the coast from where I lived. I wondered first, where would he start in a place with well over a million people, and second, how it was that I found myself in this position at this point in this man's life!?

By the time we had arrived at the bus station outside of the town that I lived, it was too late to arrange a ticket, and driving him on to PE seemed to me unwise as he would have had nowhere to stay and little time to find something as the night approached. Others had deemed my alternative decision to be equally unwise. But I could not deny the report the inner ear of my heart delivered to my mind, "I came for the sick." The decision was made. What was supposed to be less than a two-hour drive to bring a man home, turned into weeks of two strangers getting to know each other in close quarters, as we took the exit and apprehensively landed at my humble bachelor pad in Jeffreys Bay.

He looked to me for answers. I quickly ran out of cheap words and finally, got honest and confessed that I had no answers. We had already gone to PE several times over in a bid to find his mother, which was entirely nonsensical, yet we did it, because what else could we do? On occasion, I would walk into the horror scenes you might expect to find with a man whose organs seemed to be failing, with nowhere to run because this was where I lived. It was a single bedroom open-plan pad with no door that divided my room from the living space. Because of this, there were nights that I would be startled awake to find this stranger standing next to my bed, crying over me because he was scared. Scared of dying. Scared of dying horribly. Scared of never seeing his daughter again. And scared, it seemed, almost to death, of being alone through it all. I, as well, was terribly scared. Scared of what was going to become of this man in my care.

It is easier to recognize when a man has come to his end, when it is accompanied by very evident physical difficulties. There seemed to me actual evidence that physically, this road that he was on was one of suffering. It was more than that, though. In his speech, I could find no hint of hope. It was no secret that this man had found his end. But because I had my health, you needed to look deeper in me to find out that I too was at my wit's end.

By no means were we on the same battlefield, but I could not handle the difficulty of this situation any longer. I ate the rotten fruit of comparison and felt I would be a fraud to complain about my difficulties when held up against his. So I kept quiet. I was totally unqualified. There was no end in sight and all that I had to offer were conversations about the love of God and His nearness to us in times of crisis. It appeared to be meaningless to this man because he felt his entire life had been lived in crisis and never had a sense of God's nearness in it. This time was no different. The hospitals were not helping, and although the community around me supported us so well with food parcels, prayer, wisdom, and counsel, even one of my friends managed to get him on antiretroviral therapy medication which felt like our greatest victory, still, he had not the eyes to see that this support was in fact God's nearness. Even though we were learning to celebrate the minor victories as we went, it never took long for the different kind of weight of trying to be someone's savior to crush me.

I cried out to God. I could not do it any longer. Being the good Samaritan was too hard to sustain. It was during this time when I started to fathom the weight of their yes when my brother and his wife lovingly obeyed Jesus and took me in. When there is no end in sight, no knowledge of how long, ahead of you only the unknown that is riddled with risk, it is unnerving. I had learned, that by acknowledging that I myself need The Good Samaritan, that is Jesus, it changed the way that I moved as a good Samaritan. It dawned on me that these utterances that I had been hearing, "I came for the sick", pointed not only to my friend who needed the Great Physician, it highlighted the state of my own heart. He came for us both. My heart was sick and needed to be operated on. It was not a question of whether I should or should not do good works, the question was, what, or who was resourcing the works that I do. This "honorable" account of me trying to help someone was, in fact, not noble at all. I had been deceived and was trying to earn my keep in the Father's house. Indeed, I was trying to be someone's saviour, and it would surely crush me.

"My son, you do not have to do this. I will love you the same. But would you?"

Those were the words in thought that welled up from the deepest part of my being that changed everything. It set me free. Onto a path of wanting nothing less than to keep going. The spirit of adoption had breathed wind into my sails, graciously reminding me of my true identity and divine place of belonging. Whatever the result of this effort to help, it would not jeopardize my position in Christ. The love of the Father had moved me from duty to delight.

"The moment Jesus came up out of the baptismal waters, the skies opened up and he saw God's Spirit—it looked like a dove—descending and landing on him. And along with the Spirit, a voice: 'This is my Son, chosen and marked by my love, delight of my life.'" (Matthew 3:16-17)

I knew well the things that my heart had been complaining about during this time. I was grumbling. But legalistically, I refused to quit. I was scared, angry, and falsely believed that my sonship was being threatened by my imminent failure in attempting to be someone's saviour. That was why when I had been quickened to read this portion of Matthew's Gospel, my heart came undone, as I heard that I am the Fathers delight, chosen by Him and marked by His love, that I am His son, despite my worried and sick heart. I couldn't believe that He would love a man like me with a heart so sick. It changed me.

From this moment onwards, the idea that my new friend might be with me for God knew how long brought with it a sense of joy. It was not just okay, it was welcomed, and as far as I could tell, absolutely necessary for the both of us.

When I saw the letter on the coffee table, it is a miracle to say that it was a moment that I had been dreading. My friend had left, and I was going to miss him terribly. He said that it was time to go. He said that he wasn't entirely sure where to go, but he knew, beyond any measure of doubt, that he was not alone. He said that God was with him.

He said God had always been with him, and now that he had the eyes to see that, he was no longer an orphan – even though he had always been a son.

He said he knew he was going to be okay.

IX

Welcome Home

Prayerfully, as I pen these last pages, a simple contribution on love, sonship, and finding our way back into the place I am not convinced we ever left, I hope that you might find yourself coming into a refreshed awareness of your divine place of belonging. For your aid, should you fall prey to the dictatorship of dubiety, the psalmist has offered for your consideration, a text that has the potential to undergird powerfully, your endeavors to wade through the weeds of worry when dealing with your doubts of belonging.

"Where shall I go from your Spirit? Or where shall I flee from your presence? If I ascend to heaven, you are there! If I make my bed in Sheol, you are there! If I take the wings of the morning and dwell in the uttermost parts of the sea, even there your hand shall lead me, and your right hand shall hold me. If I say, 'Surely the darkness shall cover me, and the light about me be night,' even the darkness is not dark to you; the night is bright as the day, for darkness is as light with you.

For you formed my inward parts, you knitted me together in my mother's womb. I praise you, for I am fearfully and wonderfully made." (Psalm 139:7-14)

Where shall we go from the Spirit that convinces us that we are the loved sons and daughters of God? The ones to whom this Kingdom legacy is bequeathed. We are heirs with Christ! Before our time, outside of time as we know it, God had you and me in mind. And before acting upon His perfect thoughts of who we are and will become, He determined it a good idea, no, a very good idea, that we should come into the world at just the precise time that He had ordained. That is a challenging thought for the soul born into a hostile, dislocated environment. But whatever the circumstances that had been waiting for us outside of the womb, before the pain, before the blessings, you and I were, and still are, fiercely loved.

Sublime is the thought, that even before the first light of our lives had been seen, He was with us in the darkness of the womb, forming our inward parts, sovereignly knitting together who we are, until His ordained due date for yours, and my arrival. And so it is, that over the long arc of time of all mankind, God Immanuel, God with us, rang true in the womb as He distinctively marked us with love for a life to be lived with Him and others.

He is all-encompassing. There is no detail too grim or too lofty that would carry the power to nullify this truth that sets us free from spiritual orphanhood. However, the difficulty lies with us. So much, if not all, of what we do has been greatly shaped by the contextual relationships that we move through life within. And because of that, we lack what we lack, because of what we have lacked. Saying it simpler, we approach God in the way in which we know Him. And how we know Him has been significantly shaped by our relationships with others.

I beg you; we cannot escape the far-reach of Jesus in this matter. There is no other solution. No greater response to our lack than that of Jesus.

"For if while we were enemies, we were reconciled to God by the death of his Son, much more, now that we are reconciled, shall we be saved by his life. More than that, we also rejoice in God through our Lord Jesus Christ, through whom we have now received reconciliation." (Romans 5:10-11)

He came that we would be reconciled back into the arms of the Father. He came to reveal the Father so that we would know Him. He came to invite us into His understanding of the relationship that He

Himself has with the Father. Some have been born into stories that imply that their very existence was not intended; that they were a mistake. Others, into steadfast and stable homes. The latter carries with it a unique set of challenges that might limit a person's understanding of the depth of the Father's love to that of their earthly example. The former has the potential of turning the idea of having a loving Father and a divine place of belonging into a toxic joke and is terribly hard to believe because of a missing father-figure in one's life. But Jesus came to divide. He drew a line down the middle and beckoned to both sides. Follow me, He said, and into the heart of the Father He would lead.

"O righteous Father, even though the world does not know you, I know you, and these know that you have sent me. I made known to them your name, and I will continue to make it known, that the love with which you have loved me may be in them, and I in them." (John 17:25-26)

With the omnipotent brilliance that He possesses, He was, and is, and will continue to be intimately mindful of the faces that make up the multitudes. As a Father who cannot lavish with love enough His sons and daughters, He gives you His undivided attention. C.S. Lewis says this, "God has infinite attention to spare for each of us. You are as much alone with Him as if you were the only being He had ever created."

Who am I that you would be mindful of me!? A moment in my life that changed me, I believe eternally, unfolded on a winter's night at a campground that I was staying at to seek God for a time. Aptly, it was named Holy Ground Camp Site. It was hidden in one of the bays along the coast of Whangarei on the north island of New Zealand. It carried with it a deep and rich history of prayer, and I was ever grateful to be given the quiet, and the beauty, to do just that. There are times in our lives when the words that we carry are filled up and discovered as if for the first time. This evening on a tiny, pebbled beach in Parua Bay, was once such moment.

I had been grappling with the psalmist's offering when he said, "Who is man that you would be mindful of him" and had wondered what it was that informed his question. Who are we that He would be mindful of us!? I believed it to be much less a question, as it was a statement of amazement that points us to God's unfailing love.

As I stood, thinking, and taking it all in, the moon-kissed silver tips of the ripples sang a gentle song as they danced across the bay. I joined in with praise as I gazed upon the heavens, the work of our great God's hands. It was as if He tilted all of existence and poured the Milky Way precisely into my eyes as I beheld the beauty that He had set in place. The Milky Way is at its best in the winter months in New Zealand, and I had the privilege of drinking it in. As my eyes drank up all that they could, He kept pouring. And pouring. And pouring.

"When I look at your heavens, the work of your fingers, the moon and the stars, which you have set in place, what is man that you are mindful of him, and the son of man that you care for him?" (Psalm 8:3-4)

As creation waits with eager longing for the revealing of sons and daughters of God, on this winter evening, it was not so much that a son had been made known to all creation; it was as if God and all creation had already known and were eagerly longing for me to catch up to the truth of it.

Our divine place of belonging is not so much a place in space or a mystical set of coordinates. That is why when in search of your God-given identity, changing the city you live in, or shifting from one church or ministry to another, or moving country in seeking this heavenly destination will prove only to be a feeble and frustrating endeavour. Our divine place of belonging is, instead, a condition. The recognition of our place of origin, in the heart of the Father, as loved sons and daughters.

We carry with us where it is that we came from. I have heard it said that believing does not make God your Father, instead your belief would give you access to the benefits of Him being your Father. I offer to you, that you have never seized to be loved. You have never seized to be His child. You have never seized to have a divine place, of divine belonging, and you have never seized to have Jesus, the One who came to reconcile you back into both.

Bless you.

NOTES

NOTES

NOTES

NOTES

NOTES

NOTES

NOTES

NOTES

NOTES

Printed in Great Britain
by Amazon